DEXTER JACKSON
and the
Tampa Bay Buccaneers

SUPER BOWL XXXVII

by Michael Sandler

Consultant: Norries Wilson
Head Football Coach
Columbia University

BEARPORT
PUBLISHING

New York, New York

Credits

Cover and Title Page, Photo by The Charlotte Observer; 4, © Michael Caulfield/WireImage.com; 5, © Donald Miralle/Getty Images; 6, Photo Courtesy Gerald Andrew Gay; 7, Photo Courtesy Gerald Andrew Gay; 8, © FSU Sports Information; 9, © Andy Lyons/Getty Images; 10, © Scott Halleran/Getty Images; 11, © David Drapkin/Getty Images; 12, © Andy Lyons/Getty Images; 13, © REUTERS; 14, © REUTERS/Pierre DuCharme; 15, © Erik S. Lesser/Getty Images; 16, © Bob Rosato/Sports Illustrated; 17, © Jamie Squire/Getty Images; 18, © Stephen Dunn/Getty Images; 19, © Ezra Shaw/Getty Images; 20, © REUTERS/Robert Galbraith; 21, © REUTERS/Robert Galbraith; 22L, © Al Bello/Getty Images; 22R, © Al Bello/Getty Images; 22 Background, © Al Bello/Getty Images.

Publisher: Kenn Goin
Senior Editor: Lisa Wiseman
Creative Director: Spencer Brinker
Design: Deborah Kaiser
Photo Researcher: Jennifer Bright

Library of Congress Cataloging-in-Publication Data

Sandler, Michael.
  Dexter Jackson and the Tampa Bay Buccaneers : Super Bowl XXXVII / by Michael Sandler.
       p. cm. — (Super Bowl superstars)
  Includes bibliographical references and index.
  ISBN-13: 978-1-59716-537-2 (library binding)
  ISBN-10: 1-59716-537-9 (library binding)
  1. Super Bowl (37th : 2003 : San Diego, Calif.)—Juvenile literature. 2. Tampa Bay Buccaneers (Football team)—Juvenile literature. 3. Jackson, Dexter, 1977—Juvenile literature. I. Title.

  GV956.2.S8S27 2008
  796.332'648—dc22

                                    2007005524

For more information, write to Bearport Publishing Company, Inc., 101 Fifth Avenue, Suite 6R, New York, New York 10003. Printed in the United States of America.

10 9 8 7 6 5 4 3 2 1

★ Contents ★

Super Bowl XXXVII (37)

It was only four minutes into Super Bowl XXXVII (37) and the Tampa Bay Buccaneers were already in trouble. The Oakland Raiders had just scored. Now they were looking to strike again. The Bucs had to fight back.

Tampa Bay charged at Oakland quarterback Rich Gannon, forcing him to make a quick throw. Bucs **defender** Dexter Jackson tracked the football with his eyes.

This ball is mine, he thought to himself.

Oakland quarterback Rich Gannon (#12) under pressure

Dexter Jackson (#34) tackles Oakland wide receiver Jerry Rice (#80).

During the 2002–2003 season, Oakland had the NFL's most powerful **offense**.

Super Bowl Dreams

While growing up, Dexter Jackson dreamed of playing in a Super Bowl. He pictured himself as a quarterback running the offense.

Offensive players are always the biggest stars. They score the points and make the TV highlights.

At Shanks High School in Florida, Dexter was a great quarterback. Dozens of college coaches wanted him to join their teams. Dexter chose Florida State University.

Dexter in his high school football uniform

Dexter signs his scholarship for Florida State University.

Dexter wasn't just a quarterback for his high school team. He was also the **punter** and **placekicker**.

Making the Switch

At Florida State, however, Dexter made an unhappy discovery. The team already had several quarterbacks. If he wanted playing time, he needed to switch to defense.

Dexter found that he liked being a defender. Stopping other quarterbacks was fun. It was almost as much fun as being a quarterback.

Dexter made tackles and blocked field goals. He drove quarterbacks crazy by **intercepting** their passes.

Dexter celebrates Florida State's Orange Bowl victory in 1996.

Dexter did as well in class as he did on the football field. At Florida State, he won honors for his grades.

Welcome to Tampa

In 1999, Dexter was **drafted** by the National Football League's (NFL) Tampa Bay Buccaneers. The Bucs had once been a terrible team. They had never won a Super Bowl.

Recently, though, Tampa Bay had been getting better. Their defense was strong. Dexter joined the team as a **safety**.

Safeties are the last line of a team's defense. They tackle running backs who break free from the **line of scrimmage**. They guard players trying to catch passes.

A disappointed Bucs fan

Safeties (circled in red) begin a play a few yards behind the other defenders.

On the Move

Dexter's first few seasons weren't easy. NFL football was tougher than the college game. The players were bigger, faster, and stronger.

Each week, Dexter improved. The team was getting better, too. They made the playoffs in 1999, 2000, and 2001.

Still, fans wanted more. They dreamed of seeing the Bucs play in a Super Bowl. Would their dream ever come true?

Dexter (#34) stops Baltimore Raven Terry Allen (#29) during a game in 2001.

As the Bucs got better, fans finally had something to smile about.

In 1999, Dexter's first season with Tampa Bay, the team reached the conference championship game. However, the St. Louis Rams beat the Bucs and kept them out of the Super Bowl.

13

The Special Season

Throughout 2002, Dexter made one big play after another. In September, he had a key interception against the St. Louis Rams.

Then in October, he slammed into an Atlanta Falcons **receiver**, knocking the ball loose. It popped into the hands of Dexter's teammate Dwight Smith for a game-changing **turnover**.

Finally, in November, he intercepted a pass from Green Bay Packers quarterback Brett Favre. Dexter returned the ball for 58 yards (53 m). The Bucs roared into the playoffs!

Dexter tries to keep his balance after intercepting a pass from Rams quarterback Kurt Warner.

Dexter (#34) slams into Falcon Brian Kozlowski (#85), who fumbled the ball.

In 2002, Tampa Bay had the league's best defense. They gave up fewer points than any other NFL team.

The Defense Delivers

In the first game of the playoffs, Tampa Bay crushed the San Francisco 49ers. As usual, the defense was amazing. Dexter and his teammates didn't allow a single touchdown.

Next up were the Philadelphia Eagles. The Bucs had lost four straight games to them. This time, however, Tampa Bay shut down the Eagles' offense in a 27-10 victory. For the first time in history, Tampa Bay was going to the Super Bowl.

The Bucs score a touchdown against the San Francisco 49ers.

Bucs quarterback Brad Johnson (#14) gets ready to hand the ball to his teammate during the game against the Eagles.

During the game against the Eagles, it was 26°F (3°C). The Bucs had never won a game in such a cold temperature.

Ready for the Raiders

The Bucs' **opponents** in Super Bowl XXXVII (37) were the Oakland Raiders. Stopping Oakland quarterback Rich Gannon was Tampa Bay's final test. Could Dexter and his teammates meet the challenge?

The answer was yes. At the end of the first quarter, Dexter **picked off** one of Gannon's passes. Then late in the second quarter, he did it again. Dexter was becoming a nightmare for the Oakland quarterback.

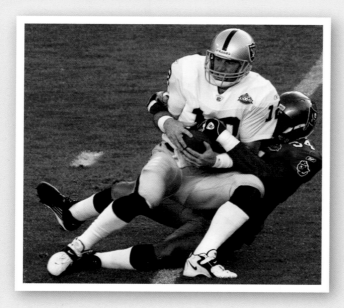

Rich Gannon (#12) gets sacked by Bucs defensive end Greg Spires (#94).

Dexter was the first player ever to make two interceptions in the first half of a Super Bowl.

Dexter (#34) intercepts a pass.

Winners

In the second half of the game, Dexter's teammates kept the **pressure** on Gannon. Three times Tampa Bay defenders intercepted his passes. Each time they ran all the way back for touchdowns.

Midway through the third quarter, Tampa Bay led by 31 points. At game's end, the scoreboard showed Tampa Bay 48, Oakland 21. The Bucs were finally Super Bowl champions!

Bucs cornerback Dwight Smith runs the ball for a touchdown after intercepting it from quarterback Rich Gannon.

Dexter was voted Super Bowl **MVP**. He was the first safety to win the award in 30 years.

Dexter and his MVP trophy

★ Key Players ★

There were other key players on the Tampa Bay Buccaneers who helped win Super Bowl XXXVII (37). Here are two of them.

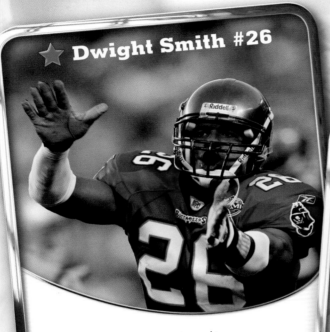

Dwight Smith #26

Position:	Cornerback
Born:	8/13/1978 in Detroit, Michigan
Height:	5' 10" (1.77 m)
Weight:	201 pounds (91 kg)
Key Plays:	Ran 2 interceptions back for touchdowns

Brad Johnson #14

Position:	Quarterback
Born:	9/13/1968 in Marietta, Georgia
Height:	6' 5" (1.98 m)
Weight:	225 pounds (102 kg)
Key Plays:	Passed for 215 yards (197 m) and 2 touchdowns

★ Glossary ★

defender (di-FEND-ur)
a player who has the job of stopping the other team from scoring

drafted (DRAFT-id)
picked after college to play for an NFL team

intercepting (*in*-tur-SEPT-ing)
catching a pass thrown by the other team

line of scrimmage (LINE UHV SKRIM-ij) an imaginary line across the field where the ball is put at the beginning of a play

MVP (EM-VEE-PEE)
the most valuable player in a game or season

offense (AW-fenss)
the players on a football team whose job it is to score points

opponents (uh-POH-nuhnts)
athletes who people play against in a sporting event

picked off (PIKT AWF)
intercepted; caught a ball meant for a receiver

placekicker (PLAYSS-*kik*-ur)
a player who kicks the ball for field goals, extra points, and kickoffs

pressure (PRESH-ur)
burden or strain on a player

punter (PUHNT-ur)
a player who drops the ball and kicks it to give possession of the ball to the other team

receiver (ri-SEE-vur)
a player whose job it is to catch passes

safety (SAYF-tee)
a defensive player who lines up farther back than other defensive players

turnover (TURN-*oh*-vur)
a play that results in the loss of the football to the other team

Bibliography

George, Thomas. "Jackson Was the Surprise Inside the Box." *New York Times*, January 28, 2003.

St. Petersburg Times (Florida)

www.buccaneers.com

www.NFL.com

Read More

Giglio, Joe. *Great Teams in Pro Football History*. Chicago, IL: Raintree (2006).

Goodman, Michael E. *The History of Tampa Bay Buccaneers*. Mankato, MN: Creative Education (2004).

Johnson, Brad, and Greg Brown. *Play with Passion*. Kirkland, WA: Positively For Kids, Inc. (2004).

Learn More Online

To learn more about Dexter Jackson, the Tampa Bay Buccaneers, and the Super Bowl, visit **www.bearportpublishing.com/SuperBowlSuperstars**

Index